PAWNEE

Big Buddy Books
An Imprint of Abdo Publishing
abdopublishing.com

Katie Lajiness

abdopublishing.com

Published by Abdo Publishing, a division of ABDO, PO Box 398166, Minneapolis, Minnesota 55439.
Copyright © 2019 by Abdo Consulting Group, Inc. International copyrights reserved in all countries. No part
of this book may be reproduced in any form without written permission from the publisher. Big Buddy Books™
is a trademark and logo of Abdo Publishing.

Printed in the United States of America, North Mankato, Minnesota.
052018
092018

THIS BOOK CONTAINS
RECYCLED MATERIALS

Cover Photo: Rick Ryan/rickryan56.wixsite.com/rickryan.
Background Photo: Arina P Habich/Shutterstock.
Interior Photos: Dan Thornberg/Getty Images (p. 19); Getty Images (p. 23); gnagel/Getty Images (p. 30); Hi-Story/
    Alamy Stock Photo (p. 13); J Pat Carter/Getty Images (p. 5); Marilyn Angel Wynn/Native Stock (pp. 9, 15, 16, 17,
    25, 26, 29); mlharing/Getty Images (p. 11); Rastan/Getty Images (p. 21); sharply done/Getty Images (p. 27).

Coordinating Series Editor: Tamara L. Britton
Contributing Editor: Jill Roesler
Graphic Design: Jenny Christensen, Maria Hosley

Library of Congress Control Number: 2017962685

Publisher's Cataloging-in-Publication Data

Name: Lajiness, Katie, author.
Title: Pawnee / by Katie Lajiness.
Description: Minneapolis, Minnesota : Abdo Publishing, 2019. | Series: Native Americans
    set 4 | Includes online resources and index.
Identifiers: ISBN 9781532115110 (lib.bdg.) | ISBN 9781532155833 (ebook)
Subjects: LCSH: Pawnee Indians--Juvenile literature. | Indians of North America--
    Juvenile literature. | Indigenous peoples--Social life and customs--Juvenile literature.
    | Cultural anthropology--Juvenile literature.
Classification: DDC 970.00497--dc23

CONTENTS

Amazing People

Hundreds of years ago, North America was mostly wild, open land. Native American tribes lived on the land. Each had its own language and **customs**.

The Pawnee (paw-NEE) are one Native American tribe. Many know them for their **ceremonies** and handmade crafts. Let's learn more about these Native Americans.

Did You Know?

The name *Pawnee* means "horn." The name came from the men's hairstyle, which looked like a horn.

Today, the Pawnee attend ceremonies to honor their native customs. The social dance is one of the few where men and women dance together.

Pawnee Territory

The Pawnee lived in four groups called bands. They were the Wolf, the Grand, the Republican, and the Tappage.

Three of the four bands lived along the Arkansas River in Kansas. They became the Southern Pawnee. The Wolf band was the Northern Pawnee. They moved north to the Platte River in present-day Nebraska.

CANADA

UNITED STATES

PAWNEE HOMELANDS

NEBRASKA

IOWA

KANSAS

MISSOURI

MEXICO

7

HOME LIFE

Most of the year, the Pawnee lived in villages with ten to 12 roundhouses. Tribe members used dirt, grass, and branches to build a rounded shelter.

Hunters left their villages about two times a year to follow the buffalo. During hunts, the men stayed in teepees. That is because teepees were easy to put up and take down.

The Pawnee also lived in earth lodges. They used logs, branches, plants, and mud to build the dome-shaped buildings.

9

What They Ate

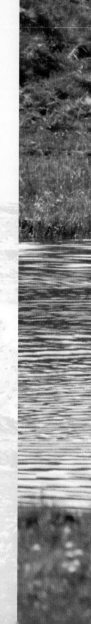

Pawnee women grew beans, corn, squash, and sunflowers. Men hunted buffalo and antelope. Once the Pawnee captured horses, they could hunt farther away from the village.

Hunters drove buffalo into swampy areas where it was easier to hunt them.

DAILY LIFE

Pawnee dressed like other tribes on the Great Plains. Women decorated their dresses with beads and paint. Men wore war shirts as a sign of their strength during battle. Over time, the Pawnee began to wear European clothes such as vests and boots.

Pawnee men shaved their heads except for a small piece on top. Then they added grease and paint so their hair stood up like a horn.

Women and men had different jobs. Women took care of the crops and made clothes. They also made pottery.

Men worked in one of three groups. Some were **medicine** men, some were warriors, and others were hunters.

Pawnee women used stone bowls to mash berries and medicine.

MADE BY HAND

The Pawnee made many objects by hand. They often used natural supplies. These arts and crafts added beauty to everyday life.

Pawnee Dice
The Pawnee made dice from fruit seeds and painted characters on them. They used the dice to play games.

Pawnee Headdress

Tribe members wore headdresses during celebrations. Women added paint and sewed beads into the headband.

Pawnee Hand Drum

The Pawnee stretched rawhide over a wood bucket to make a drum. Then they painted designs on the top.

Moccasins

To make moccasins, women sewed beads onto the elk hide.

Spirit Life

The Pawnee believed in balancing life between the gods and nature. **Ceremonies** included songs, poems, and dances.

The people called **medicine** men Shamans (SHAH-mans). These men helped treat illness and protect against enemies.

Many of the Pawnee ceremonies were about corn. This crop was a blessing from the sun god.

STORYTELLERS

Stories were important to the Pawnee. In one story, a woman took care of a spotted pony that later turned into a man. The woman fell in love with the horse man and they ran away together.

Years later, the tribe found the woman in the wild. She had given birth to many spotted ponies. The tribe believed this is how spotted ponies came to exist.

Tribe members celebrated the sun, moon, and stars. They believed that some of the stars were gods.

FIGHTING FOR LAND

Throughout history, the Pawnee lived in peace among the new settlers. The tribe helped settlers fight other Native American tribes. These included the Sioux, Cheyenne, Arapaho, Kiowa, and Comanche tribes.

Pawnee and Sioux in battle

Zinpka Mato.

 Artwork shows famous battles between the Sioux and the Pawnee.

The US government asked the Pawnee to sign several **treaties** during the 1800s. Over time, the tribe lost much of its land in Nebraska. Soon, the government forced the tribe onto a **reservation** in Oklahoma.

Today, the Pawnee tribal meeting hall is in Pawnee, Oklahoma.

BACK IN TIME

 1200

Pawnee entered the Great Plains from the south.

1700s

The Southern Pawnee traded many goods with French fur trappers. They traded buffalo robes and pelts for guns and tools.

1790

The tribe went from nearly 10,000 to about 2,200 after many died of illnesses.

1874

Settlers pushed the Pawnee out of Nebraska and into Indian Territory.

1883

The Women's National Indian Association began a group on the Pawnee reservation. They wanted to introduce the Pawnee people to Christianity.

1936

The government passed the Oklahoma Indian Welfare bill into law. This allowed the Pawnee tribe to approve its own laws.

2017

Oklahoma's Pawnee Nation brought 27 different oil companies to court. The companies' way of drawing oil from the ground hurt the Pawnee's land.

THE PAWNEE TODAY

The Pawnee have a long, rich history. Many remember them as peaceful people.

Pawnee roots run deep. Today, the people have held on to those special things that make them Pawnee. Even though times have changed, many people carry the **customs**, stories, and memories of the past into the present.

Did You Know?

Today, there are between 3,000 and 4,500 Pawnee living in North America.

Pawnee artist Austin Real uses clay to make masks. He shows his artwork at fairs and craft shows around Oklahoma.

"What is life? It is the flash of a firefly in the night. It is the breath of a buffalo in the wintertime. It is the little shadow which runs across the grass and loses itself in the sunset."

— Eagle Chief Letakos-Lesa, Pawnee

GLOSSARY

celebrate to observe a holiday with special events. These events are known as celebrations.

ceremony a formal event on a special occasion.

Christianity (krihs-chee-A-nuh-tee) a religion that follows the teachings of Jesus Christ. Christians are people who practice Christianity.

custom a practice that has been around a long time and is common to a group or a place.

medicine (MEH-duh-suhn) an item used in or on the body to treat an illness, ease pain, or heal a wound.

reservation (reh-zuhr-VAY-shuhn) a piece of land set aside by the government for Native Americans to live on.

treaty an agreement made between two or more groups.

Online Resources

Booklinks
NONFICTION NETWORK
FREE! ONLINE NONFICTION RESOURCES

To learn more about the Pawnee, visit **abdobooklinks.com**. These links are routinely monitored and updated to provide the most current information available.

INDEX